IRAQ
OPERATION CORPORATE TAKEOVER

Written by:
Sean Michael Wilson

Illustrated and Lettered by:
Lee O'Connor

War on Want Content Advisers:
Nadia Idle and Ruth Tanner

Pre-press:
Ian Sharman

Production Editor:
Sean Michael Wilson

Book Design:
Lee O'Connor

Iraq: Operation Corporate Takeover
Copyright © 2007, published by War on Want / Boychild Productions Books.

War on Want
Development House
56-64 Leonard Street
London EC2A 4LT
UK

www.waronwant.org

sean-michael-wilson.blogspot.com/
www.webcomicsnation.com/boychildproductions
www.boychildproductions.co.uk

www.leeoconnor.com

www.comicspace.com/iansharman

This publication has been produced with the financial assistance of the
European Union. Under no circumstances should its contents be regarded as
necessarily reflecting the position of the European Union.

First printing: November 2007
Printed in Canada

ISBN: 0-9546596-3-5

DRAWING THE LINE

We live in a culture that carefully nurtures people into the illusionary position of claiming they're 'not interested in politics'.

But of course that in itself is a deeply political position, in which we say it's somehow OK or inevitable that three quarters of the world's population should have to live like medieval serfs beneath the smoked glass castles of the new breed of 'democratic' robber barons. As with war, 'you might not be interested in politics, but politics is interested in you'. Particularly in your passive silence, which suits the establishment just fine.

I'm no pacifist. I can see a clear moral argument for using force to protect the innocent from attack, or to help the population of a country bring down its hated dictatorship. But as the writing on the wall said during round one of the current oil war... 'WHAT IF KUWAIT PRODUCED JUST CARROTS?'

So it's deeply refreshing to see Sean Michael Wilson and Lee O'Connor turning their cartoon book X-ray vision towards the situation in Iraq, and revealing the hidden truth behind the lead wall of global spin.

Superman would be proud of them both.

Polyp

Polyp

IRAQ
OPERATION CORPORATE TAKEOVER

WRITTEN BY:
SEAN MICHAEL WILSON

ILLUSTRATED BY:
LEE O'CONNOR

9

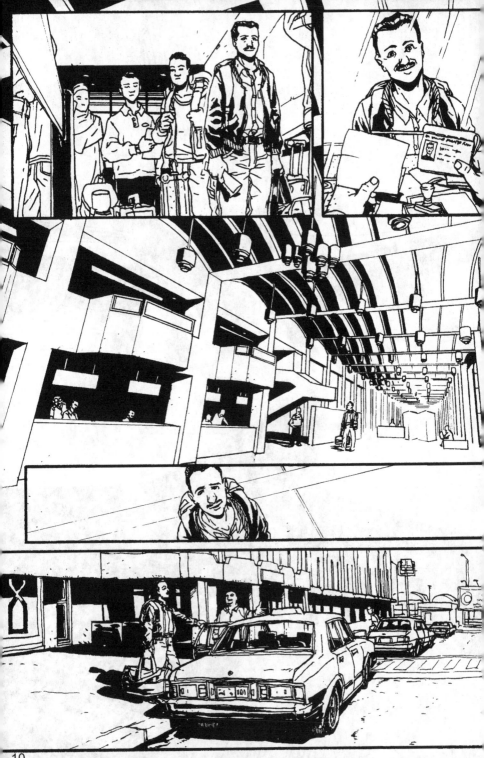

11

AH, HERE HE IS - MY SON IS BACK!

I'M GLAD TO SEE YOU GOT HERE SAFELY - LONDON IS SO FAR AWAY.

AH, IT'S NOT SO FAR DAD. ONLY A SIX HOUR FLIGHT.

NAZEM IS HERE!

12

LOOK, FATHER'S ASLEEP.

HE'S SO TIRED NOWADAYS.

IS HE ILL?

NO, BUT THERE'S A LOT OF TROUBLE WITH HIS UNION JOB. THERE'S BIG PROBLEMS WITH THE IRAQI OIL INDUSTRY.

PERHAPS HE WILL WANT TO TELL YOU HIMSELF LATER...

THERE ARE SO MANY CHANGES HERE SINCE YOU LEFT, NAZEM.

AH, THAT SOUNDS STUPID – OF COURSE THERE ARE CHANGES!

YES, I SORT OF NOTICED, SAKINA – SOMETHING ABOUT A WAR WASN'T IT?

DON'T BE SO CHEEKY!

16

21

I SUPPOSE THEY HAVE A LOT OF SCHOOLS TO FIX, SO THEY MUST BE BUSY. BUT STILL, IT'S NO GOOD MAKING THE JOB AS BAD AS *THIS*.

HAS NOBODY IN THE USA OR THE UK NOTICED WHAT A BAD JOB THESE COMPANIES ARE DOING HERE?

WELL, SOME PEOPLE HAVE NOTICED. BECHTEL HAD A $50 MILLION DOLLAR CONTRACT CANCELLED BECAUSE A US GOVERNMENT AUDIT CRITICISED THEM FOR DOING A BAD JOB.

ALSO, USAID * CLAIMED THAT COMPLAINTS FROM THE IRAQI MINISTRY OF EDUCATION SHOWED THAT ON 2% OF THE SCHOOLS THEY WERE CONTRACTED TO SORT OUT HAVE REPORTED PROBLEMS.

BUT THAT'S A DROP IN THE OCEAN - BECHTEL HAS HAD $2.85 BILLION IN IRAQ CONTRACTS!

THE AMERICAN AND BRITISH GOVERNMENTS TRY TO MAKE PEOPLE THINK THAT THEY ARE ACTING LIKE CHRISTIAN SAINTS - REBUILDING EVERYTHING AND SORTING IRAQ OUT.

THEY SHOULD SEE IMAGES OF THINGS LIKE THIS, AND REALISE HOW BAD A JOB THEY ARE DOING. I DON'T BELIEVE ITS ONLY 2% OF SCHOOLS ARE LIKE THIS. MAYBE THAT'S ALL THEY'RE ADMITTING TO.

WELL, I DON'T WANT TO TAKE THEIR SIDE, BUT THEY MUST HAVE DONE SOME THINGS RIGHT, NO?

YES, THEY HAVE - THEY GAVE THE SCHOOL A NEW COAT OF PAINT!

HA, HA!

WELL - THAT'S BETTER THAN NOTHING!

* US AGENCY FOR INTERNATIONAL DEVELOPMENT

WHAT'S GOING ON HERE?

THEY'RE KNOCKING DOWN THAT WHOLE THING, IT WAS HIT BY A BOMB. WE WERE LUCKY THAT THE SCHOOL WASN'T HIT.

HMM, THAT REMINDS ME OF SOMETHING SAMI TOLD ME.

WHO IS HE?

A FRIEND OF MINE FROM LONDON. I MEAN HE'S FROM PALESTINE, BUT I MET HIM IN LONDON.

A BIG COMPANY, CALLED CATERPILLAR FOR SOME ODD REASON, MAKES THESE HUGE BULLDOZERS, WHICH ARE USED IN PALESTINE BY THE ISRAELI AUTHORITIES.

THE ISRAELI ARMY USES THE D-9 BULLDOZERS AS MILITARY WEAPONS AND HAVE DESTROYED PALESTINIAN FAMILIES' HOUSES IN THE WEST BANK AND GAZA.... THOUSANDS OF THEM! CATERPILLAR KNOW THAT THEY ARE USED IN THIS WAY, BUT OF COURSE SELLING THE MACHINES HAS MADE THEM A HEFTY PROFIT.

LET'S SEE WHAT SAMI HAS ON HIS PALESTINE BLOG.

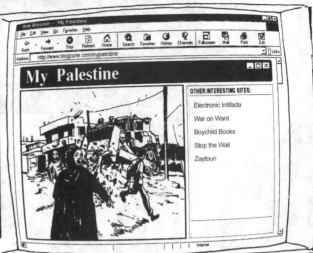

Web Browser - My Palestine

File Edit View Go Favorites Help

Back | Forward | Stop | Refresh | Home | Search | Favorites | History | Channels | Fullscreen | Mail | Print | Edit

Address http://www.blogzone.com/mypalestine

My Palestine

OTHER INTERESTING SITES:

Electronic Intifada

War on Want

Boychild Books

Stop the Wall

Zaytoun

Internet

Web Browser

Caterpillar's code of conduct says: "We believe that our success should contribute to the quality of life and prosperity of communities."

Web Browser

But in Palestine their D9 bulldozers have been used to exactly the opposite effect. The bulldozers have destroyed 11 schools in less than two months.

Web Browser

Caterpillar's bulldozers are currently also involved in one of the most controversial Israeli projects: the building of the illegal Separation Wall. It is 436 miles in length, that's the distance from London to Zurich, and 80% of it is built on Palestinian land.

DO ANY OF THE PEOPLE WHO RUN THESE COMPANIES HAVE A CONSCIENCE? HOW CAN THEY WATCH THE MONEY ROLL IN AND NOT CARE ABOUT THE DAMAGE THEY ARE DOING TO PEOPLE'S LIVES? WAR MEANS PROFIT AND THESE COMPANIES ARE MAKING A KILLING OUT OF OTHER PEOPLE'S MISERY. IT MAKES ME SO ANGRY. AND I BET THERE IS A LOT MORE TO KNOW. I HAVEN'T EVEN TALKED TO DAD ABOUT PROBLEMS WITH THE OIL INDUSTRY YET, AND I BET THEY ARE MAKING A KILLING THERE TOO.

* BASRA UNIVERSITY SUFFERED DAMAGE TO BUILDINGS, STOCK AND MORALE.
LATER, LOOTERS TOOK MANY ITEMS WHILE BRITISH SOLDIERS LOOKED ON.

I visited my sister's school this week... And saw the terrible job that the US corporation has done there. After I found out that companies like Bechtel were given the job to repair a whole load of things in Iraq's infrastructure - sewerage, electricity, health centres, the telephone system, hospitals, etc... The thing is - surprise, surprise - that Riley Bechtel, of the family that runs the company, was sworn in as one of George Bush's advisers on the Export Council to advise him on trade. So Bush bombs the hell out of Iraq, and then sends in his mates to clear it up!

But when the company got here, they realised that the scale of the clean-up was enormous and the country was in a dire state. But, of course, more chaos meant more money for the companies. In January 2004 USAID gave them another contract for $1.8 billion, almost three times the first contract.

Bechtel made a mess of it, but more importantly, they made a fortune. Many people didn't have access to drinking water, health clinics or power. Bechtel was heavily criticised, even by US groups, then at the end of 2006 Bechtel announced it was leaving Iraq. Yeah, after they sucked as much money out of us as they could!

Of course then Iraq itself was blamed for making it difficult for the companies to 'do the job', or exploit our country as I call it. But this country is under occupation by people who are best mates and working with the people who run these companies! It should be so obvious.

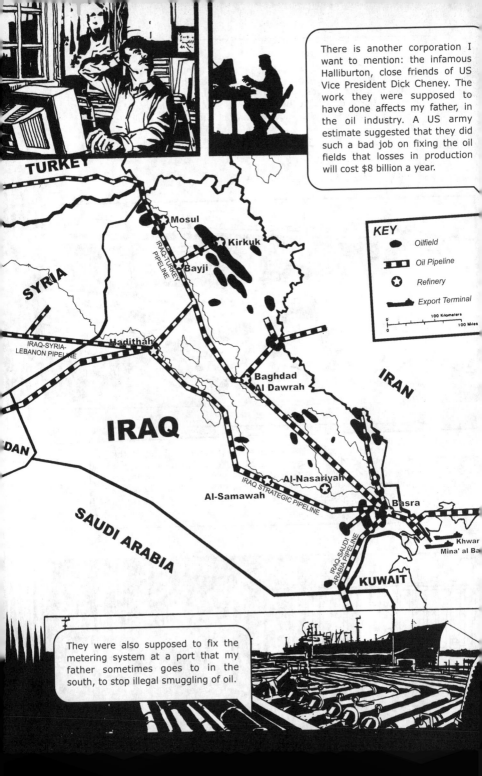

There is another corporation I want to mention: the infamous Halliburton, close friends of US Vice President Dick Cheney. The work they were supposed to have done affects my father, in the oil industry. A US army estimate suggested that they did such a bad job on fixing the oil fields that losses in production will cost $8 billion a year.

They were also supposed to fix the metering system at a port that my father sometimes goes to in the south, to stop illegal smuggling of oil.

Typically they brought in people from various poorer Asian countries to do all the dirty work for them, then didn't give them proper work benefits, while pouring vast funds into management benefits schemes instead.

The Pentagon didn't renew their contract to feed and care for the US troops in Iraq. They got $15 billion for that and still made a mess of it. How do these corporations manage to waste so much money and yet make such huge profits? The only people who are losing out here are the Iraqi people who are paying with their lives!

SORRY, THE ELECTRICITY HAS GONE. THIS HAPPENS QUITE OFTEN. PLEASE TRY BACK IN ABOUT FIVE HOURS OR SO...

PEOPLE IN THE WEST NEED TO KNOW HOW THESE COMPANIES ARE PROFITING FROM THE OCCUPATION, SO THAT THEY CAN LOBBY THEIR GOVERNMENTS.

IF MY BLOG CAN HELP TOWARDS THAT THEN I'VE DONE SOMETHING WORTHWHILE.

34

HMMM, MOTHER IS NOT HERE YET.
GO ON DAD, THIS IS INTERESTING STUFF. I MIGHT INCLUDE THIS IN MY BLOG.
OH, I'M FLATTERED MY CLEVER SON STILL LISTENS TO HIS FATHER!
OK, SO THE UK AND US GOVERNMENTS, THE INTERNATIONAL MONETARY FUND AND THE BIG OIL COMPANIES HAVE ALL HELPED SHAPE THE NEW OIL LAW IN A WAY THAT STRONGLY FAVOURS LONG TERM, EXCLUSIVE CONTRACTS FOR THESE FOREIGN OIL COMPANIES.
THIS "HYDROCARBON LAW" COULD GIVE THE FOREIGN OIL COMPANIES CONTROL OVER IRAQI OIL FOR UP TO THIRTY YEARS!

37

39

44

47

NAZEM.

WHAT'S WRONG?

KARIM, BROTHER... I WAS JUST INVOLVED IN TROUBLE WITH SOME WESTERN SOLDIERS...

SOLDIERS!

NO, NOT SOLDIERS... I MEAN THOSE SECURITY GUARDS... THOSE CORPORATE MERCENARY THUGS.

HMM, THAT SOUNDS LIKE A TYPICAL SCENE. LISTEN NAZEM, YOU HAVE TO BE VERY CAREFUL WITH THOSE PRIVATE GUARDS. THEY'RE A LAW UNTO THEMSELVES.

I'LL TELL YOU SOMETHING THAT HAPPENED INVOLVING THEM.

49

HE DIED WITHIN A FEW MINUTES.

HIS FAMILY HAVE BEEN TRYING FOR MONTHS NOW TO GET SOME KIND OF JUSTICE FROM THE CONTRACTORS WHO EMPLOY THESE MERCENARIES, BUT THERE DOESN'T SEEM TO BE ANYBODY WHO CAN PIN THEM DOWN.

THAT'S RIGHT! – THEY'VE GOT IMMUNITY FROM IRAQI LAWS. THEY'RE ACCOUNTABLE TO NO ONE.

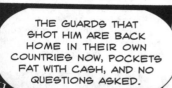

THE GUARDS THAT SHOT HIM ARE BACK HOME IN THEIR OWN COUNTRIES NOW, POCKETS FAT WITH CASH, AND NO QUESTIONS ASKED.

Private Military and Security Companies (PMSCs) sell security and military services around the world. These mercenary groups have brushed up their image and moved into the corporate boardroom, becoming a 'normal' part of the military sector. The PMSC industry comprises hundreds of companies operating in more than fifty countries worldwide. They have grown exponentially in recent years due to the occupation of Iraq, which has allowed British mercenaries to reap huge profits. This has allowed the British PMSC sector to grow into a multi-billion dollar industry.

The UK government has failed to enact laws to punish their human rights abuses. No prosecutions have followed hundreds of accounts of personnel from private military and security firms committing abuses in Iraq.

A website run by a former employee of the UK-based Aegis Defence Services showed security guards randomly shooting automatic rifles at civilian cars. Aegis is led by Lieutenant-Colonel Tim Spicer, who broke a UN arms embargo on Sierra Leone with his former company Sandline International, and was jailed in Papua New Guinea for earlier activities.

Human rights abuses by private military companies' personnel have also included torture, rape, humiliation and using dogs to terrify prisoners in the Abu Ghraib prison in Iraq, as well as earlier involvement in rape and prostitution rings in Bosnia. Tough legislation is needed as a matter of urgency to ban the use of mercenaries in these conflict situations.

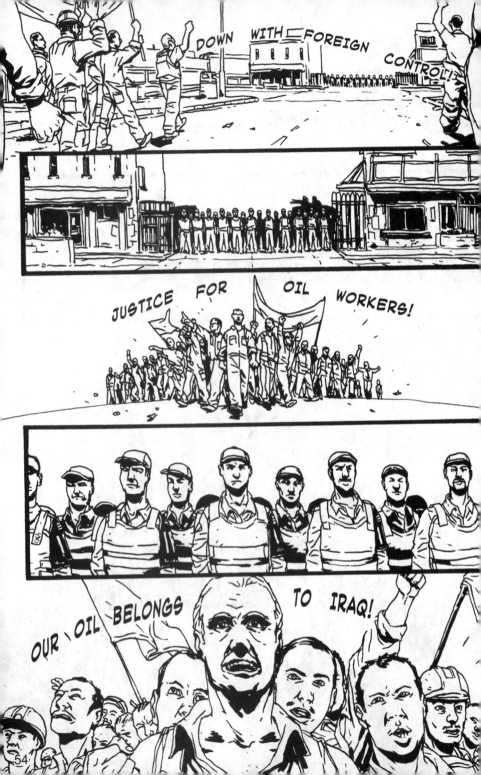

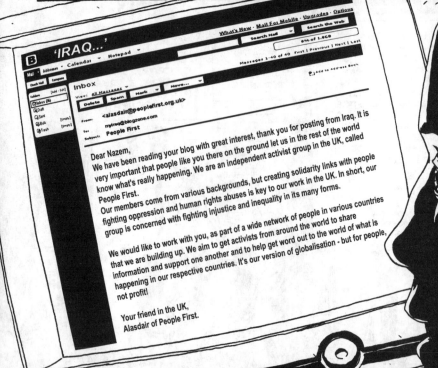

Dear Nazem,

We have been reading your blog with great interest, thank you for posting from Iraq. It is very important that people like you there on the ground let us in the rest of the world know what's really happening. We are an independent activist group in the UK, called People First.

Our members come from various backgrounds, but creating solidarity links with people fighting oppression and human rights abuses is key to our work in the UK. In short, our group is concerned with fighting injustice and inequality in its many forms.

We would like to work with you, as part of a wide network of people in various countries that we are building up. We aim to get activists from around the world to share information and support one another and to help get word out to the world of what is happening in our respective countries. It's our version of globalisation - but for people, not profit!

Your friend in the UK,
Alasdair of People First.

OVER TEN THOUSAND
VISITORS ALREADY –
WOW!

I DIDN'T THINK IT WOULD
BE SO MUCH. THIS IS
GREAT. ALASDAIR AND
THIS 'PEOPLE FIRST' GROUP
SEEM REALLY INTERESTING.
INTERNATIONAL SUPPORT...
I'M HELPING THEM GAIN
INFORMATION AND WE ARE
ALL FIGHTING THE SAME
INJUSTICES TOGETHER.
YES, THIS IS WHAT I NEED!

HMM, PEOPLE FIRST...
GOOD NAME – AND
THAT'S EXACTLY IT!

WE NEED A SYSTEM THAT
PUTS PEOPLE FIRST... BUT
THE ONE WE'VE GOT PUTS
PROFIT FIRST. THAT'S WHAT
ALL THIS STUFF COMES
DOWN TO. AFTER ALL THE
POLITICS, ECONOMICS,
OIL, BATTLES, MASS MEDIA,
ETC, IT'S ALL ABOUT MONEY.

IT ALL COMES DOWN TO:
PEOPLE OR PROFIT, WHICH
SIDE ARE YOU ON?

e your blog

Blog title	IRAQ: OPERATION CORPORATE TAKEOVE

ress ... .blogzone.com

The End... of the beginning.

War on Want

Poverty is political. The only way to tackle poverty is to look at the roots of why people are poor in the first place. War on Want tackles the structures that keep poor people poor. We focus on the fact that the decisions taken by politicians in rich countries can mean life or death for people in developing countries. And in many cases these decisions serve the interests of big business rather than the world's poor.

We have the power to reshape the global landscape - to ensure that people across the world can live in justice and peace. We all need to use the power at our disposal to change the way the world works.

War on Want is part of a global movement fighting for a fairer world. War on Want fights poverty in developing countries in partnership and solidarity with people affected by globalisation. We work with some of the bravest and most inspiring groups in the world. In rural communities, in factories and sweatshops, in conflict zones and on the margins of society, we work with people fighting for real, lasting change.

War on Want campaigns for workers' rights and against the root causes of global poverty, inequality and injustice. From trade rules rigged in favour of rich countries and their multinational companies to human rights abuse in Palestine and Iraq, War on Want campaigns in the UK and internationally to deliver real lasting change.

War on Want's Corporations and Conflict campaign

The cost of war

War is one of the chief causes of poverty. War can completely undermine a country's development prospects, destroying schools and hospitals and putting agricultural land out of use for years to come. 80% of the world's 20 poorest countries have suffered a major war in the past 15 years, and the human legacy of war continues long after. Nine of the 10 countries with the world's highest child mortality rates have suffered from conflict in recent years.

The relationship between corporations and conflict

Not everyone is made poorer by war. Many companies thrive off conflict, whether through supplying military hardware to armed forces or running mercenary armies on behalf of combatant states. Others fuel conflict through their operations in war zones, such as oil companies in volatile countries like Colombia and Iraq, or through their continued trade in goods such as blood diamonds. Others profit from financing the war effort.

The economic orthodoxy of the society we live in starts from the premise that corporations, through the free market mechanism, both thrive in and create environments of peace, harmony and stability. If only everyone could surrender to the benign presence of the global corporation, all would be right in the world.

The widely acknowledged economic motives behind the recent war in Iraq have dented this paradigm in society at large. As oil, arms, private security and many other industries plundered Iraq's economy, it became clear that companies often profit from war and conflict. Claims of corporate influence at Washington suggest that some companies go so far as to fuel conflict for their own ends. And even those companies which claim they are merely restoring commerce and production to a war-ravaged economy are unable to deny that they themselves are dependent on security apparatuses complicit in human rights abuses, in turn fuelling violence and poverty.

Over the last 10 years, in response to pressure from campaigners, many of the world's largest companies have adopted 'codes of conduct' which govern their behaviour towards their workforce, local communities, the environment and others affected by their operations. The problem is that these codes are entirely voluntary, with few monitoring mechanisms and no means of independent enforcement.

UK government policy

Corporations do not produce the society we most want to inhabit; they produce one which allows them to maximise profits. In the UK we have a legal framework which restricts what companies can do. Globally there is no such framework. Without this legal restriction corporations will continue to make profits whatever the cost, even where those profits are built on conflict and poverty.

That is why War on Want is calling for the establishment of a global regulatory framework to force companies on the world stage to abide by the same types of law that companies in the UK have to follow. This requires a major change in attitude on the part of the UK government, which has steadfastly opposed international calls to hold companies accountable for their activities overseas. By contrast, it prefers to support the voluntary approach of 'corporate social responsibility', despite the fact that this has been shown to be an ineffective alternative to regulation.

Campaigning for change

War on Want exists not merely to document problems across the world. Through War on Want's partners among grassroots organisations in Asia, Latin America and Africa, we aim to redress some of the damage that Western behaviour inflicts on the world. Aggressive corporate behaviour is not tolerated passively – it is resisted by a myriad of groups working their way out of poverty. These groups need our solidarity.

Iraq: Operation Corporate Takeover forms part of War on Want's Corporations and Conflict campaign to confront those companies which profit from war. This campaign complements War on Want's longstanding support for our partners in conflict zones: some of the world's bravest men and women, on the front line in the struggle for human rights.

The aim of the campaign is to expose the many different ways in which the corporate sector is involved in conflict, and to suggest public action to call such companies to account. This is War on Want's mission more widely: to support people in developing countries in their struggle for survival, but also to inspire people in rich countries to challenge the root causes of poverty around the world.

War on Want's work in Palestine

Palestine is facing an unprecedented humanitarian crisis. The UN reports that 70% of Palestinians in the West Bank and Gaza are now living in acute poverty, a figure comparable to poverty levels in sub-Saharan Africa. Over 50% are now dependent on food aid.

This poverty is a direct result of 40 years of Israeli occupation. According to the UK government's Department for International Development: 'Poverty in the Occupied Palestinian Territories is a product of occupation and conflict.' Only by ending the occupation can the root causes of poverty be addressed.

War on Want supports grassroots organisations struggling for Palestinians' rights. We put pressure on the British government to end the injustice and support the Palestinians' right to self-determination and a life of dignity and peace.

Corporate complicity in Israel's crimes against the Palestinian people

War on Want believes that companies must be brought to account for their complicity in Israel's crimes against the Palestinian people. Ultimately there must be a binding international framework of regulation to ensure corporations' accountability for their activities around the world. In all three of the following cases, the companies in question are helping to create 'facts on the ground' which will preclude any possibility of a viable Palestinian state. They can be considered complicit in the violation of Palestinians' human rights as a result of their operations in occupied Palestinian territory. Yet Western governments have failed to take any action to stop corporate involvement in the occupation of Palestine, even though they have an obligation to do so under the Fourth Geneva Convention. It is left up to individuals to take action and call such companies to account.

Stop the Wall

Israel has confiscated thousands of acres of fertile Palestinian land in order to build its illegal Separation Wall. The UN estimates that 60% of farming families are now cut off from their land due to lack of permits. Palestinian homes, farms and water systems have been purposefully destroyed.

The Wall is nearing completion, despite the International Court of Justice's 2004 ruling that it is in contravention of international law. When finished, the Wall will be 703km (436 miles) long. That's the distance from London to Zurich. Human rights are being violated on a daily basis, while restrictions on movement have devastated the Palestinian economy and created a series of impoverished ghettos. There are currently over 500 checkpoints and physical obstacles restricting Palestinian movement within the West Bank. As former UN Secretary-General Kofi Annan confirmed, 'The Israeli closure system is a primary cause of poverty and humanitarian crisis in the occupied Palestinian territory.'

www.stopthewall.org

Construction, destruction

The bulldozers of well-known Western companies such as Caterpillar, Volvo and Daewoo are being used by the Israeli army to destroy Palestinian homes, schools, orchards and olive groves, and their machines are building Israel's illegal Separation Wall. The United Nations has singled out Caterpillar in particular for its complicity in the violation of Palestinian human rights.

From settlement to shelf

Israel has built an extensive network of settlements on land which it captured during the 1967 Six Day War. There are currently 135 official settlements in the West Bank and occupied Jerusalem, plus a further 100 unofficial settlements, or 'outposts'. These settlements are now home to over 450,000 Israelis, whose towns and cities are built on occupied Palestinian territory and who farm many thousands of acres of the best Palestinian land.

Many of Britain's high street stores - including Tesco, Waitrose, Sainsbury's, Selfridges and Argos - stock goods which have been produced in Israeli settlements within occupied Palestinian territory. These settlements represent the physical reality of the Occupation as experienced by Palestinians on a daily basis, and export revenue is important to their economic sustainability. Stores which sell settlement produce are thereby supporting the Occupation.

Connex and the annexation of East Jerusalem

Connex is a familiar name to commuters in south-east England, having run trains in and out of London for seven years before its franchise was terminated for poor financial management in 2003. Less well known is that Connex is the central partner in a new $500 million light rail system designed to link Jerusalem to the illegal settlements of the occupied West Bank. As such the company is playing a key role in Israel's attempt to make its annexation of the Palestinian territory of East Jerusalem irreversible, thereby undermining any chance of a just peace for the Palestinian people.

War on Want's work in Iraq

Hands Off Iraqi Oil

Military occupation and daily violence are not the only threats the people of Iraq face today. The new Oil Law being considered by Iraq's parliament could give foreign oil companies contracts to extract Iraqi oil for a generation. War on Want believes that long-term contracts concerning Iraq's oil should not be signed while the country is still under occupation.

Halliburton

The company that has profited most from the invasion of Iraq is US Vice-President Dick Cheney's former firm, Halliburton, with contracts worth over $10 billion. The company is currently the subject of multiple criminal investigations into overcharging and kickbacks, much of which is related to their abuse of 'cost-plus' contracts. In 'cost-plus' contracts, profits are calculated as a percentage of expenses. The more money a contractor spends on the contract, the more profit they make, leaving the contracts open to massive abuse. Overcharging by the company has run from ordering specially embroidered towels to charging extortionate prices for petrol.

Iraq's oil reserves are the second largest in the world, and oil is central to the country's economy, accounting for 95% of all government revenue.

Decisions on the future of the oil industry are therefore fundamental to Iraq's future, and should be made by the Iraqi people without outside interference. Yet the US and UK governments, international oil companies and the International Monetary Fund have all played key roles in shaping the new oil law.

Ordinary Iraqis and Iraqi civil society, meanwhile, who overwhelmingly oppose it, have been excluded from the process.

Iraqi Federation of Oil Unions

War on Want supports organisations in conflict zones such as the Iraqi Federation of Oil Unions (IFOU). Despite threats to its members' security, the IFOU raises awareness in Iraq and abroad of the dangers of the draft oil law and fights for the rights of oil workers.

The IFOU is based in Basra, one of the poorest areas of Iraq. The situation for the oilworkers in the region is worsened by the fact that the US used depleted uranium extensively in and around the oil fields during the first Gulf War, which continues to damage Iraqis' health and places people's lives at risk.

War on Want supports the IFOU in its fight against privatisation and its campaign for international solidarity for the plight of the oilworkers. Posters are being distributed, educational materials produced and public meetings held to raise awareness amongst the Iraqi people of the issues surrounding oil privatisation and working conditions in the industry.

Foreign parties with vested interests are exploiting the vulnerability of an Iraqi government facing ongoing military occupation and constant security threats.

War on Want believes that Iraqi oil belongs to the Iraqi people. Decisions on the future of the oil industry should be made by the Iraqi people without outside interference.

Production Sharing Agreements (PSAs)

The development model being promoted in Iraq, and supported by key figures in the Oil Ministry, is based on contracts previously known as production sharing agreements (PSAs). Oil experts agree that their purpose is largely political: technically they keep legal ownership of oil reserves in state hands, while practically delivering oil companies the same results as the concession agreements they replaced.

War on Want's analysis shows that PSAs would have four major disadvantages for the Iraqi people:

1) Iraq would lose an enormous amount of revenue (making it conversely highly profitable for the foreign companies);

2) The terms of the contracts would be agreed while the Iraqi state is very weak and still under occupation, but be fixed for 25-40 years;

3) PSAs would deny Iraq the ability to regulate or plan its oil industry, leaving foreign companies' operations immune from future legislation;

4) PSAs would shift decisions on any disputes out of Iraq into international arbitration courts, where the Iraqi constitution, body of law and national interest are simply not relevant.

> **Bechtel**
>
> In its survey of American construction company Bechtel's work to renovate Iraqi schools, the US military reported a list of complaints from staff at Iraq's Education Ministry as follows: 'Major clean-up work required; Bathrooms in poor condition; the new fans are cheap and burned out immediately upon use. All inspected were already broken; Lousy paint job,' and concluded that: 'Most schools were strewn with refuse everywhere, had toilets that didn't work.' This was part of a major reconstruction contract awarded to Bechtel worth $1 billion. Bechtel has also been accused of failing to follow through with its contract to repair Baghdad's sewerage system. One year into the contract, increases in the incidence of cholera, kidney stones and diarrhoea have all been blamed on Bechtel.

Private Military and Security Companies

There are hundreds of Private Military and Security Companies (PMSCs) operating in more than 50 countries worldwide. They work for governments, international institutions and corporations. PMSCs have grown exponentially in recent years. They enable governments to cover their tracks and evade accountability; they are not accountable to government or the public and so allow governments to get round legal obstacles. PMSCs have become so much a part of the war effort that major Western countries, like the UK and US, would now struggle to wage war without PMSC partners.

PMSC activity in Iraq

While Iraq means bloodshed and death on a massive scale to most people, to PMSCs it has represented a boom time. Iraqi contracts boosted the annual revenue of UK PMSCs alone from £320 million in 2003 to more than £1.8 billion in 2004. The potential for human rights abuses in such situations is an ever-present threat, yet it is nearly impossible to hold PMSCs to account.

At Abu Ghraib prison, employees of two PMSCs (Titan and CACI) were implicated in the abuse-of-prisoners scandal. A 'trophy video' of a former employee of UK PMSC Aegis showing corporate mercenaries randomly shooting automatic weapons at civilian cars in Baghdad is only one of hundreds of reported incidents of contractors firing indiscriminately at civilians. Despite these cases and many more, no private military contractor has been prosecuted throughout the war in Iraq.

The UK government demonstrated that it was acutely aware of many of the problems posed by PMSCs when it published its Green Paper on regulating the sector in 2002. However, five years on the UK government has failed to introduce legislation to take forward any of the options presented in the Green Paper. War on Want believes that the UK government must move towards legislation to control the PMSC sector as an urgent priority. Legislation must outlaw PMSC involvement in all forms of direct combat and combat support, understood in their widest possible senses. Self-regulation by the industry is not an option.

Take Action

There are many positive actions you can take to help bring about justice for the people affected by these corporate crimes.

Activism

● **Order a Corporations and Conflict War on Want action pack:**
This pack contains reports, action cards and other materials which will inform you about the issues and get you started on taking action

● **Become a War on Want activist:**
Get more involved in our campaigns, set up meetings or events in your local area to create awareness and encourage activism around these issues. Order a number of materials action cards, stickers, posters and leaflets -- that you can give out on your campus, in your workplace or local area. Contact us at *yan@waronwant.org*

● **Join War on Want:**
Help us support our partners on the ground and campaign in the UK for better regulation of corporate activities. Visit *www.waronwant.org/joinus*

Actions on Palestine

● **Call for the suspension of the EU-Israel Association Agreement:**
The agreement gives trading preferences to Israel despite its human rights abuses against the Palestinian people. Its suspension would bring pressure on Israel to abide by international law.

● **Email the Foreign Secretary**

● **Email your MEP**

● **Write to the companies involved:**
Express your concern that these companies are supporting the illegal occupation of Palestine. Details can be found on page 12 of War on Want's free-to-download-report Profiting from the Occupation at
www.waronwant.org/palestine

● **Buy Zaytoun fairtrade olive oil:**
Help undo the damage caused by Caterpillar's bulldozers. Zaytoun is a UK-based non-profit project to purchase pesticide-free extra virgin olive oil from Palestinian farmers at fair trade prices. Olive oil is the backbone of the Palestinian agricultural economy, but over half of the country's olive harvest goes unsold and spoils.

Actions on Iraq

● **PMSC regulation:** Write to the Foreign Secretary, to call on the Government to move towards binding legislation to control the PMSC sector.

● **Oil theft:** Write to your MP and ask them to write to the Foreign Secretary about UK government involvement in selling off Iraq's oil. At time of printing the Oil Law had not yet been passed. To find out latest actions to lobby MPs and companies involved in the contracts visit *www.waronwant.org/iraqoil*

To find out about your MP and other representatives contact details visit
www.theyworkforyou.com

Why support War on Want?

1. We tackle the root causes of poverty and human rights abuses, not just the symptoms

We believe that global poverty and human rights abuses can only be eliminated by changing the structures that cause poverty and abuse in the first place, like unfair trading systems and exploitative business practices. We tackle these root causes head on, pioneering campaigns against issues such as corporations profiting from conflict in the developing world and the uncontrolled liberalisation of global trade policies, and we lead the way in bringing these injustices to a wider audience.

We are at the centre of the NGO campaigning network in the UK, standing up for the rights of the most vulnerable and pressing for genuine solutions, whatever the cost.

2. We work hand in hand with our partners

We believe that people living in poverty are best place to find sustainable solutions to better their situations. We partner directly with grassroots organisations in the developing world and work alongside them in their struggle for their rights. Our partners' activities and needs directly inform our work and campaigning here in the UK. The focus of our overseas activity is on helping people secure the right to decent work, as we believe that this is one of the most fundamental human rights and a highly powerful tool in the reduction of poverty and social exclusion.

3. We will spend your money effectively

We are not a huge organisation, and we make every effort to keep our administrative and fundraising costs to a minimum. Consequently more of your money goes directly towards our campaigning work and to support our project partners.

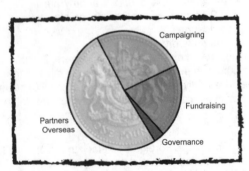

In the year ending 31 March 2007, for every pound donated we spent:
- 51p on tackling the needs of our partners overseas;
- 26p on campaigning against the root causes of global poverty;
- 20p on fundraising, so that we can continue our work in future; and
- 3p on governance

Biographies

Sean Michael Wilson is from Edinburgh, Scotland but is now living in Japan. He studied Psychology and Sociology at Glasgow, Edinburgh and London Universities. His first published story came out in 1998 in a book and display of an exhibition of comic art in London. His work includes the graphic novel ANGEL OF THE WOODS, the story CHIMPIRA in MANGA MOVER, the poem comics in BEAUTIFUL THINGS, the historical manga THE JAPANESE DRAWING ROOM (with artist Sakura Mizuki, of THE RING horror manga) and a manga on a late 19th Century writer: LAFCADIO HEARN'S JAPANESE GHOST STORIES.

He is currently working on a comic book to be published in Japanese. As well as writing comic books he has also made several cultural documentaries that have been shown on British television. Comic book writing though is closer to his heart. His comic/manga influences include Alan Moore, Grant Morrison, Eddie Campbell, Jiro Taniguchi and Yoshihiro Tatsumi. Others: Jorge Luis Borges, Franz Kafka, John Lennon, Magick, the Marx Brothers, Terence Stamp, Scott Walker...

Lee O'Connor is the grinning farmboy who graduated from the UK's only Comic Illustration university course some nineteen years after he started drawing at the age of one year old. He has worked on film, illustration, artwork, murals and has lectured both at home and abroad. He lives in rural Devon, England. Lee's influences include, but are by no means limited to; Yoshiyuki Sadamoto, Nicola Mari, Paul Grist, Jean Giraud and Mark E. Smith. Notable comic work includes DINNER GUESTS in the PROPHECY ANTHOLOGY - which appears alongside work by some of the brightest stars in alternative comics - SPACE DOUBLES from Th3rd World, COMMERCIAL SUICIDE, VURT: THE COMIC REMIX, many small press titles and the ongoing self-published series CONTRACT BLUES. He even had a drawing of a jellyfish dressed as Groucho Marx published in cult British comic 2000AD. Lee is always working on new projects and his website can be reached at: **www.leeoconnor.com**

Lee would like to thank Ron Tiner, Andrew 'Roge' Rogers, TEAM, The Totnes and Swinedown Massives, Ma, Pa, Bruv and Sildy for their invaluable assistance in bringing this book to print.